PROFILES

Elizabeth Fry

Angela Bull

Illustrated by
Edward Mortelmans

Hamish Hamilton
London

Titles in the Profiles *series*

Edith Cavell	0-241-11479-9	Montgomery of Alamein	0-241-11562-0
Marie Curie	0-241-11741-0	The Queen Mother	0-241-11030-0
Roald Dahl	0-241-11043-2	Florence Nightingale	0-241-11477-2
Thomas Edison	0-241-10713-X	Emmeline Pankhurst	0-241-11478-0
Anne Frank	0-241-11294-X	Pope John Paul II	0-241-10711-3
Elizabeth Fry	0-241-12084-5	Anna Pavlova	0-241-10481-5
Indira Gandhi	0-241-11772-0	Prince Philip	0-241-11167-6
Gandhi	0-241-11166-8	Beatrix Potter	0-241-12051-9
Basil Hume	0-241-11204-4	Lucinda Prior-Palmer	0-241-10710-5
Helen Keller	0-241-11295-8	Viv Richards	0-241-12046-2
Amy Johnson	0-241-12317-8	Barry Sheene	0-241-10851-9
John Lennon	0-241-11561-2	Mother Teresa	0-241-10933-7
Martin Luther King	0-241-10931-0	Queen Victoria	0-241-10480-7
Nelson Mandela	0-241-11913-8	The Princess of Wales	0-241-11740-2
Bob Marley	0-241-11476-4		

HAMISH HAMILTON CHILDREN'S BOOKS

Penguin Books Ltd, 27 Wrights Lane, London W8 5TZ (Publishing & Editorial)
and Harmondsworth, Middlesex, England (Distribution & Warehouse)
Viking Penguin Inc., 40 West 23rd Street, New York, New York 10010, U.S.A.
Penguin Books Australia Ltd, Ringwood, Victoria, Australia
Penguin Books Canada Limited, 2801 John Street, Markham, Ontario, Canada L3R 1B4
Penguin Books (N.Z.) Ltd, 182-190 Wairau Road, Auckland 10, New Zealand

First published in Great Britain 1987 by
Hamish Hamilton Children's Books

British Library Cataloguing-in-Publication Data:
Bull, Angela
Elizabeth Fry. – (Profiles).
1. Fry Elizabeth – Juvenile literature
2. Prison reformers – Great Britain – Biography – Juvenile literature
I. Title II. Series
365'.7'0924 HV8978.F7
ISBN 0-241-12084-5

Typeset by Pioneer
Printed in Great Britain at the
University Press, Cambridge

Contents

Elizabeth Fry

1 The Gurneys of Earlham

Earlham was like a house in a story book. Built beside a river, with sweeping lawns and avenues of trees, it was large, rambling and ancient. Within its rosy brick walls, rooms with strange names – the Blue Room, the Chintz Room, the Ante Room Chamber, the Great Room – were jumbled higgledy-piggledy. They were linked so that a child could run the whole length of the house without using any of its winding passages. Half-secret staircases dropped through the thickness of the walls; eighty-eight cupboards were tucked into dark corners and behind fireplaces; while high under the roof was the queer Eleven-sided Room, all slopes and angles and shadowy alcoves.

Special houses should have special families, and in this Earlham was lucky. In the year 1786 Mr John Gurney moved there with his wife and eight small children. By 1791 there were seven girls and four boys to explore the gardens, row boats on the river, and play hide-and-seek amongst the rambling rooms and the eighty-eight cupboards.

John Gurney was a rich man. He owned a bank in nearby Norwich, for in those days banks were private businesses, even issuing their own banknotes. He was a handsome, jolly father, who adored his family. Mrs Gurney too was kind and sweet, but with such a big household of children and servants to manage, she was often tired and preoccupied.

The eldest child was Catherine, usually called Kitty. In a good-looking family she was the plainest, but she was warm-hearted, clever, and much loved by the others. Pretty, lively Rachel followed her, and then timid, delicate Betsy. John, the handsome eldest son, came next and then four younger sisters. They were slim, hazel-eyed Richenda who had a talent for art; Hannah, the most beautiful of the girls; Louisa, the cleverest and sharpest-tongued; and gentle, quiet Priscilla. Last came three more boys – Samuel, Joseph and Daniel. In appearance they were all tall and fair; in character they were active and vivacious. Chatter and laughter rang through the maze of rooms from daybreak till nightfall.

In November 1792 a sudden hush fell over Earlham. Mrs Gurney had been taken ill. Eighteenth-century doctors could do little, and soon the family knew that she was dying. Shut up in the nursery, the children waited in misery. They heard that their mother had struggled out of bed to pray on her knees for sixteen-year-old Kitty who would have to take charge of her brothers and sisters; for John, her beloved eldest son; and for bright little Joseph. The others seemed to have been forgotten. At last the nursery door opened, and their father came in. There was no need for words. His sad face told them that their mother was dead.

Mr Gurney did all that he could to make up for his

Earlham, the Gurneys' home

children's loss. He showered them with presents – toys, ponies, books of music. To hide the emptiness at the centre of their home, he filled the house with guests. Children came to play, and young men to dance and flirt with the girls. Gaiety soon returned to Earlham, and in all the neighbourhood there was no family so popular and talked about as the Gurneys. They picnicked, sang, climbed haystacks, built bonfires, and raced their ponies over fields and commons

There was a reckless streak in the young Gurneys. They seemed to enjoy danger. Once, the seven girls joined hands across the main road, to stop the mail coach as it galloped towards Norwich. There they stood, their red cloaks fluttering in the breeze, waiting for the coach as it thundered up the road, laden with passengers and mail bags. They were confident that the horses would not charge into a line of people. The coachman, who had seen them with horror, felt the coach lurch to a halt just in time. The girls were triumphant, but people in the neighbourhood shook their heads over such wild behaviour.

Even an indulgent father like John Gurney saw that children needed lessons as well as fun. The girls got up at six, and worked in the Schoolroom, with Kitty as their teacher. Later they sewed, while Kitty read history aloud to them. They all kept lengthy diaries, and studied music and art. 'Fixing the plan of piano practice is an important thing,' Richenda wrote in her diary. 'The instrument hardly ever ceases for five minutes.' But there was still endless time to chat, ride, and enjoy themselves; and why should girls worry about education? They all hoped to marry. None of them would need to have a career, or earn her own living. Such things were unheard of for girls like the Gurneys.

On the whole they lived in the typical manner of wealthy country families, but in two ways they were different. Firstly John Gurney was not the usual kind of country Squire. He was a businessman, who only rented Earlham, so he felt no responsibility for the poor people in the village outside his gates. He didn't even know their names. And this was partly because of the second difference. The Gurneys never attended the church on the edge of their grounds. They were Quakers.

The Quakers were a strict, rather isolated group of

Christians. They had been founded a hundred years earlier by George Fox, who wanted to get back to the simpler ways of the first Christians. People only needed to gather without fuss, pray in silence, and share their experiences of God.

Fox put forward his ideas soon after the Civil War in which Englishmen had fought for their religious beliefs. The ruling classes, who mostly belonged to the Church of England, feared that other religious groups might cause trouble again, so when they heard about the Quakers, they framed harsh laws against them. For unity and mutual protection, the Quakers closed ranks in a self-contained body, with its own ways and manners, which lasted long after the persecutions were over.

By 1790 the Quakers seemed to outsiders a solemn, rather odd collection of people. They believed in simplicity, so wore plain, drab clothes, and called each other 'thee' instead of 'you'. They condemned most pleasures as distractions from the serious things of life. At their Sunday meetings they were silent, or spoke in everyday words which they felt were inspired by God.

The lively Gurney children, with their bright clothes, their games and parties, knew quite well that they were not like most Quakers, but they were bound by family tradition. Their parents and grandparents had all been Quakers. So, on Sunday mornings, cross and miserable, the children trailed off to the meeting house in a Norwich back street called Goats Lane. There they suffered, sitting on hard benches, while elderly Quakers droned on about the sinfulness of dances and short-

The meeting house in Goats Lane

sleeved dresses. After two hours, the relief of coming out into the fresh air was enormous.

A favourite word among the Gurneys was 'dis', meaning disgusting. 'Goats was dis,' they wrote, Sunday after Sunday, in their diaries.

2 Betsy

Amongst the children of a big family, there is sometimes one who is a misfit. With the Gurneys it was Betsy.

Her real name was Elizabeth, and she was born on 21 May 1780. She came third after Kitty and Rachel, who were such a close pair that a younger sister tagging onto them was often a nuisance. And Betsy was unlike Kitty and Rachel and the others in character. While they were cheerful, confident and healthy, she was anxious, easily frightened, and frequently ill.

Safety and happiness for Betsy meant being with her mother, but she could never be more than one small item among Mrs Gurney's many concerns. Secretly she longed to be an only child, as baby after baby arrived to crowd her still further into the background. With an uncanny premonition of disaster, she feared that her mother might die, and sometimes crept to her bedside when Mrs Gurney was asleep, to make sure she was still breathing.

Sleep, for Betsy, was another thing to be dreaded. Ever since a seaside holiday, when their nurse had foolishly ducked her in the sea, she had suffered from nightmares about drowning. She often dreamed she was standing alone on a rock as the waves rose higher and higher, dashing over her, and at last sucking her down into their icy depths. Loud noises terrified her too. She would never go near her father's sporting guns. Worst of all were the dark rooms of Earlham. When her sisters and brothers played hide-and-seek, squeezing into cupboards, burrowing under the flounces of the four-posters, and crouching in the corners of the sinister Eleven-sided Room, Betsy could hardly bear it. At bedtime she begged for a light in the room, but the sisters who slept with her were scornful. The nurse refused to allow it, although Betsy woke night after night, choking and screaming from that terrible dream about the sea.

Nobody understood her. None of the other children were nervous, yet Betsy's fears and anxieties often made her ill. Presently she found there was a kind of pleasure in illness. She could be alone – a rare treat in that large household – tucked up in bed in calm daylight, listening to the games, the piano practice, the scampering feet along the winding passages, and know that for once she need not join in. As Betsy's delicacy became an established fact, she was allowed to sleep on in the mornings when her sisters got up. Her ailments were dosed with laudanum, a popular drug, which left her feeling slow and drowsy. But then there were more worries, for her younger sisters outstripped her in lessons. Betsy, who never cared much for books, was labelled stupid as well as timid and sickly. She really was the odd one out, in that laughing, lively, active family.

Her mother's death, when she was twelve and a half,

Mr and Mrs Gurney

was an appalling blow. Always Betsy had longed for some special motherly cherishing. Now the chance had gone for ever. Mrs Gurney had not even remembered her name in her last prayer. Betsy grew more and more depressed, solitary and unwell. 'Betsy is so ill, I look forward with most gloomy thoughts concerning her,' wrote Louisa in her diary, with more excitement than sympathy. 'Dearest Betsy, she seems to have no one for her friend, for none of us are intimate with her.'

But there were times when Betsy shook off her moods. She certainly took part in stopping the mail coach. She loved music and dancing, and with her sensitive nature was extremely responsive to them. At a party she could suddenly light up, sparkle, talk and dance with as much brilliance as attractive Rachel. Betsy had beautiful manners too. Unable to bear being hurt herself, she

Betsy dressed for a dance

shrank from being hurtful or unkind to anyone else. All the Gurneys were polite in company, however much they might tease each other in private; but Betsy's politeness had an extra fastidious refinement. When she rose above her depression, and forgot to compare herself gloomily with her sisters, she behaved with the charm of a fairytale princess.

Betsy was tall, with blue eyes and long, pale golden hair, parted in the middle. The clothes girls wore at that time – airy muslin dresses, with low necks and high waists – suited her slender, graceful figure. So although there were admirers of Kitty and Rachel among the young men invited to Earlham, Betsy was the first to receive a proposal. She was only fifteen when James Lloyd asked her to marry him.

James Lloyd was the son of another rich Quaker banker. Staying at Earlham in the summer of 1795, James fell in love with Betsy, as she did with him. There was a brief engagement, and then, for reasons now unknown, it was broken off. Possibly her father decided she was too young to marry, but Betsy was ill for months afterwards with depression and disappointment.

While she lay upstairs, nursing her wounded heart, her sisters gathered on the lawn, or in the great bow window of the Ante Room, eagerly discussing what had happened. How extraordinary that such a thing should happen to Betsy, the strange, moody sister, the odd one out! And if Betsy guessed that they were gossiping about her, perhaps the unfamiliar importance gave her a little comfort.

3 A Division in the Family

Betsy was often too unwell to attend Sunday meetings at Goats Lane. She didn't mind. 'Goats' was just as 'dis' to her as it was to her sisters. Yet as she lay in bed, or sat brooding in her favourite spot, the low window-seat in the Blue Room which looked over an avenue of lime trees, religious ideas gradually began to take possession of her mind.

An ancestor of her mother's, Robert Barclay, was famous for giving the first complete account of Quaker beliefs in his book, *An Apology for the True Christian Religion*, published in 1676. Something of his seriousness seemed to have been inherited by Betsy. She was a serious girl.

The record of this can be found in Betsy's surviving diaries, which begin in April 1797, just before she was seventeen. She used the diary more to examine her conscience than to describe what she did, and she soon found a problem to struggle with. Young Prince William Frederick, a nephew of the King, was a soldier stationed in Norwich. John Gurney was introduced to him, and invited him to dinner at Earlham. A warm friendship sprang up between the Prince and the Gurneys; and Prince William kept his carriage waiting

In the window-seat in Earlham

in the Earlham drive while he lingered for another song, another dance, or the fun of seeing mischievous Rachel acting out a Quaker meeting.

Betsy loved these occasions, but they worried her too. She described her excitement and how music and compliments carried her away. Then she scolded herself because enjoyment always led to sins of vanity and selfishness.

None of her sisters reacted like this. They laughed and danced with untroubled minds. Betsy felt cut off from them, and perhaps a little superior, as she tried to work out for herself the rules of right behaviour. She felt that a religious faith might be a help in her difficulties, if only she could find one.

Early in 1798 the Gurneys heard that a well-known Quaker from America, William Savery, would be at the meeting at Goats Lane on 3 February. Betsy was not excited by the news. Her thoughts might be turning to religion, but she expected nothing from 'Goats'. With the excuse of stomach-ache, she almost stayed at home. At the last minute she changed her mind. She had some new scarlet boots with purple laces which she wanted to wear. With her colourfully dressed sisters, Betsy rustled into the front row of the meeting.

William Savery, middle-aged and sober, was shocked by the Gurneys' finery, but he soon forgot it. He stood up and began to speak. In 1798 England and France were at war. The country hummed with talk of battles and invasions. To Savery this seemed wrong. He spoke instead of the blessings of peace, love and brotherhood. For the first time at 'Goats', Betsy's heart was touched. A tear slid down her cheek, and she felt that this was the message she had been waiting for all her life.

After the meeting she was unexpectedly invited home by her uncle, Joseph Gurney. He and his family were strict Quakers, wearing plain clothes, using plain speech, and disapproving of John Gurney's children. But he must have noticed that Betsy was different, for she alone was asked to come back to his house, and dine with William Savery. Betsy felt painfully conspicuous in her scarlet riding habit and purple-laced boots, but it was worth the embarrassment. She listened so eagerly to Savery's talk that, when it was time for the evening meeting, Uncle Joseph suggested that she and Savery should drive alone together to 'Goats'.

Although two thousand people had assembled to hear William Savery, it was the drive before the meeting that Betsy always remembered. 'We had much serious talk,' she recorded in her diary. 'What he said to me was like a refreshing shower on parched up earth.' He spoke again of the peace and joy of lives dedicated to God, and Betsy went home in a turmoil. She had never known such inspiration; and it had come from a Quaker!

William Savery was invited to Earlham, and immediately liked the Gurneys. If they had not been so wealthy, they could have been good Christians, he thought. Betsy hurried to 'Goats' next Sunday, but, to her dismay, Savery had left for London. The meeting was as dull as ever. Afterwards the admiring stares of some officers pleased her, and then she felt guilty about being vain. How she wished she could be like Savery, but it was very hard. She felt torn apart by all her conflicting thoughts and wishes.

John Gurney decided she needed a holiday, and suggested London. There would be balls and theatres, and – what most delighted Betsy – Savery would be there. Late in February, she and her father left Earlham in their silk-lined carriage. With her poke bonnet and muff Betsy looked outwardly demure, but inside she was bubbling with excitement.

After quiet Earlham, and countrified old Norwich, London seemed huge, dark with smoke, and very frightening. Everyone knew how crime-ridden the streets were. Timid Betsy was afraid a thief might pounce on her. She took laudanum and brandy to calm her nerves.

The relations she was staying with were determined to give her a good time. They took her to plays, encouraged her to dress fashionably, and introduced her to some agreeable cousins. But Betsy was bored by the theatre, disliked having her hair done up with feathers, and preferred Savery even to her handsome cousin Hudson Gurney. Her relations teased her about her passion for this middle-aged man in Quaker clothes, but Betsy didn't care. What mattered were the ideals of goodness she was learning from him.

When, after seven weeks, she returned to Earlham, her sisters were horrified. Betsy had become so grave and pious. Her bright clothes were left in the cupboard, and she made excuses not to join in the family music. Tauntingly they inquired if she had fallen in love with Savery. 'No,' said Betsy. 'I love him as a person without being in love.'

In her diary she confided a strange effect of Savery's teaching about peace. 'I dreamed the sea as usual was coming to wash me away, but I was beyond its reach. Since then I do not remember having that dream again. Odd!'

But the old family happiness was disturbed. Betsy and her sisters were growing further and further apart. Once again a holiday seemed to John Gurney the best way of resolving things. The family set off on a long journey to visit more relations. Unfortunately Betsy continued to irritate her sisters. She wouldn't dance, or go to a military review because she disapproved of war. They, in turn, irritated her because they wouldn't go to Quaker meetings, or sympathise with the mental conflicts she was going through.

In September the family reached Coalbrookdale, the

Betsy in her plain Quaker clothes

home of cousin Priscilla Gurney. She was a plain Quaker, living simply, and dressing only in black. Just to be with her gave Betsy a sense of peace. One Sunday she introduced Betsy to a woman called Deborah Darby, one of a family of iron manufacturers who had refused to make weapons for the war with France. Betsy revered Deborah's attitude, and something about Betsy caught the older woman's imagination. As they talked, a few days later, Deborah made a strange prophecy.

'You will be a light to the blind,' she told Betsy, 'speech to the dumb, and feet to the lame.'

4 Joseph Fry

The question for Betsy was how Deborah Darby's prophecy could ever be fulfilled. Opportunities for women hardly existed. Either they married, or they lived at home as old maids. They certainly didn't go out into the world, trying, in some unspecified way, to be a light to the blind. Yet it was very exciting to be the subject of such a prophecy; and, coming from Deborah Darby, it confirmed Betsy's belief that her first step should be to become a true Quaker.

Back at Earlham she exchanged her fashionable muslin dresses for brown and grey ones with high necks and natural waistlines. She wore a white handkerchief round her throat, and a white cap on her head. Anyone who saw her would know she was a Quaker, and so would not expect her to dance or sing. The plain Quaker speech made life easier too. She had to think before she spoke, and she could stop herself rushing into arguments or flirtations. She tried, as well, to get up early, to read more and improve her education. She also struggled to overcome her fear of darkness by going alone round Earlham at night, without a lamp, forcing herself to climb narrow staircases, and enter the ghostly Green Room, or the dreadful Eleven-sided Room.

If Betsy overdid the plain Quakerism, it was a reaction against her family's disapproval. They were not reconciled to her new ways, and Kitty would not even let her speak about religion to her younger sisters. Perhaps that was why Betsy started looking outwards from Earlham.

The villagers living beyond their beautiful grounds were strangers to the Gurneys. As a religious duty Betsy began to visit them, and she was shocked. How could she have lived for years in comfort, with these poor creatures so near at hand! The cottages were cold and bare; the people hungry, dirty and ignorant.

Reading to a little boy from the village

Hardly knowing how best to help them, Betsy began reading Bible stories on Sunday evenings to one little boy. No one had ever read stories to him before. He told his friends, and next week a group had gathered. Boldly Betsy led them up to the Eleven-sided Room, where they sat on the floor, listening. Every week more children came, and presently Betsy was obliged to move them to the Laundry, a large out-building which was usually empty since the Earlham washing was only done once a month.

Now on winter Sundays, while her family sat by the fire, Betsy was out in the freezing Laundry with seventy children, some sickly, some starving, some crippled by factory work. They looked terrible, and smelled worse. 'Betsy's Imps,' her sisters scornfully called them. Yet Betsy found these evenings intensely satisfying. Without quite knowing how, she kept the children happy and attentive. She read and explained the stories to them in her musical voice. They listened, and came back for more.

The following summer Betsy's brother, John, invited a Quaker acquaintance, Joseph Fry, to stay at Earlham. He too came from a wealthy family, but he wasn't handsome and elegant like the Gurneys. He was a thickset, young man, who dressed in plain Quaker clothes. Betsy's sisters were quick to comment on his long nose, lisp and braying laugh. He was musical, but that was about all that could be discovered in his favour by the Gurney girls.

Yet, like James Lloyd four years earlier, he seemed drawn to Betsy. She looked cool and pure beside her

Joseph Fry

brightly dressed sisters. On 27 July he asked her to marry him. Betsy declined. She realized that he would be a good match in terms of money and position, but neither he, nor the idea of marriage, attracted her. She continued with her Imps and her programme of self-improvement. But Joe Fry didn't forget her. In December he wrote to John Gurney. Could he see Betsy again?

John Gurney agreed, and on 17 December Betsy came in from riding to find Joe by the fireside, round-shouldered and awkward, but gazing at her adoringly. It was, she confessed in her diary, an agitating time. She talked to him, and found him surprisingly sympathetic. She explained her sense of vocation, and her wish to work for the good of others, and asked how these could be combined with the household duties of a married woman. Easily, Joe replied. If she were his wife, he would give her every freedom. It was tempting, but Betsy wasn't in love with him. She refused his second proposal.

Still Joe didn't give up. When, in the spring of 1800, Betsy stayed in London again, she met him everywhere. She liked him as a friend; she dreamed pleasantly of him, which was a good sign. But she was a stronger character than he was, and his doglike devotion could be exasperating. Family pressure, however, was swinging against her. The Gurneys had decided that marriage with a plain Quaker would be the best thing for Betsy. When she returned to Earlham, he was asked to follow her.

'I begin to wish for his arrival,' Betsy wrote in surprise on her twentieth birthday. Did she love him, or not? She couldn't make up her mind. At last Joe forced the decision upon her. He showed her a gold watch, and told her that he would leave it in the garden next morning. If she picked it up, it would be a sign that she accepted him. If she didn't, he would go away for ever.

Joe laid the watch on a white seat, in a little garden bordered by three high walls and a shrubbery. He didn't know that six mischievous sisters were hiding in the bushes. They saw Betsy approach the seat, pause, turn away, creep back, and hesitatingly pick up the watch. Without saying a word, she had chosen to be Joe's wife.

The wedding day was 19 August 1800. She and Joe

The wedding at Goats

stood side by side in 'Goats', holding hands as they made their vows to each other in the Quaker style, with no clergyman to conduct the service. Other Quakers rose to pray for blessings on the couple, and then the Frys drove back to Earlham for the reception. 'The day passed off well,' Betsy wrote in her diary, 'although cold hands and a beating heart were often my lot.'

But altogether she was glad to leave the difficulties of life with her family, and start afresh with a husband who had promised her freedom to follow her vocation.

5 A Married Woman

Within a few weeks Betsy's hopes were fading. Marriage had not brought her freedom; not at all.

Joe took her to live in London, in the heart of the dark, smoky city. The Frys were bankers and traders, and Betsy's new home in St Mildred's Court was hemmed in by the offices of the business, and by warehouses full of tea, coffee and spices, whose odours filled the narrow courtyard. Unmarried clerks clattered upstairs to sleep in her attics; wagons were loaded and unloaded under her windows. It was very different from Earlham.

Joe's brother, William, had previously occupied the house, and when he moved out, nobody got it ready for the young couple. Arriving from her honeymoon, Betsy was horrified by the mess. She sat in a hastily arranged parlour, trying not to feel depressed.

Next day was Sunday, and there were more shocks. Nearby, in Gracechurch Street, was the Quaker meeting house which many of the Frys attended. As they came out, they headed for St Mildred's Court. It was the custom for all members of the family – aunts, uncles, cousins, and those more distantly related – to have dinner there on Sundays. No one had warned Betsy, and her housekeeping seemed in tatters as dozens of Quakers poured in, staring at her critically, munching their food, and settling down for afternoon naps in whatever corner suited them.

Betsy had resolved to love Joe's parents, but it was difficult. The Frys prided themselves on their plain, blunt ways, and they soon let Betsy know that she seemed to them ridiculously polished and elegant, and not like a Quaker at all. Even Joe, in his home surroundings, complained that her manners had 'too much of the courtier about them'. Politeness was as natural to Betsy as breathing. She couldn't change, even to please these awkward new relations.

London Quaker society, of which the Frys were leading members, was stuffy and narrow-minded. Betsy attended her first Sunday meeting with high hopes, but she found Gracechurch Street quite as 'dis' as 'Goats' had been. There the Quakers sat, mulling over trivialities of dress and behaviour. No one suggested that a religious gathering should have a spiritual purpose.

Betsy longed for spiritual growth. It was part of the freedom Joe had promised. She persuaded him to read the Bible with her in the mornings, but he was lazy about getting up, and then he had to hurry to his office, so the readings were brief. Besides, Quakers didn't normally do that kind of thing. It made Joe uncomfortable.

All day long Betsy was occupied. There were the servants to organise, a task she dreaded, and other Quakers visited constantly, to sit with her through long afternoons and evenings, full of heavy, moralising talk. She and Joe were hardly ever alone. Presently she found she was expecting a baby. She was pleased, but children would fetter her still more; and how would she ever be a light to the blind with so many people pressing in upon her? Altogether her first year of marriage was a disappointment.

Her baby, Katharine, was born on 22 August 1801. When Betsy took her back to Earlham, her perspective changed. Her father was delighted with his grand-daughter. Her sisters, who had visited St Mildred's Court, and found it unbearable, welcomed her warmly. Poor Betsy, they thought. London Quaker life must be terrible! But Betsy was amazed by the Earlham atmosphere of idle enjoyment. No one had even troubled to go on reading to her poor Imps. She was glad when it was time for her to go home.

Eight years passed. Still the traders' wagons rumbled, and the spice scents drifted in with the London fogs. By 1809 Betsy had five children. She was no longer a slender girl, but tall and imposing in her Quaker cap and plain silk dresses. People were beginning to call her by her real name, Elizabeth. And still the feeling nagged that life should be more than just a round of home duties and Sunday meetings.

In 1809 Joe's father died, and things improved. Joe inherited old Mr Fry's country home, Plashet, in Essex. They moved out of London, and Elizabeth seized new opportunities for charitable work such as she had begun once at Earlham. While Joe landscaped the gardens, and the children rode their ponies, Elizabeth visited the local cottages, helping the sick, starting a school, and in winter turning a barn into a soup kitchen where hungry people were given meals.

At last she had some of the freedom Joe had promised, since they were too far out of London to be

Visiting the poor

burdened with his relations. They were not a close couple, but Joe's money was available for Elizabeth's charities; and he didn't complain about all the time she spent with her poor neighbours. There were eight children by 1812. Elizabeth meant to be a good mother to them, but other activities interested her more. She was becoming known as a Quaker speaker, and often travelled to address distant meetings. Every day she bustled about, trying to do good.

Yet she was aware that, somehow, she was failing. In helping the poor at Plashet, she was only scratching at the surface of a huge problem of nationwide poverty; and she seemed to have little influence over her own family. Joe was becoming indifferent to religion. Her children were downright rebellious. After hearing a Quaker meeting castigating parted hair, her eldest girls had rushed straight home and parted theirs. Elizabeth didn't know how to control them. She suspected that eyebrows were being raised at Earlham over her naughty children. Kitty and Rachel hadn't married, but Hannah and Louisa had large families of children who always behaved beautifully. Louisa had even written a book on the subject.

'I feel my life is slipping away to little purpose,' she wrote sadly in her diary. It looked as if Deborah Darby's prophecy would never be fulfilled.

Then, in October 1812, Joe brought home bad news. The war with France had caused a financial crisis. The Frys' bank was in trouble, and the upkeep of Plashet was expensive. They would have to leave, and move back to London.

6 Newgate

London in 1812 was a strange mixture of grandeur and squalor. In their spacious houses the rich and aristocratic dined, waltzed, and gambled away fortunes at cards. The poor were crowded into filthy, undrained slums, and they never enjoyed a good dinner. The war had caused enormous price rises. Bread had never cost so much, and hundreds of people were literally starving to death. If some turned to crime, it was hardly surprising.

For that was what was happening. Crime figures, like food prices, were soaring. Thieves and pickpockets lurked in every street, highwaymen terrified the countryside, forgery and murder were common, drunkenness was rife, and thousands of people were seriously in debt. The authorities met the situation by imposing stricter and stricter penalties. Criminals were imprisoned, beaten, or put in the stocks, and for over two hundred offences the punishment was death. A child as young as ten could be hanged merely for stealing a pair of stockings.

The problem of crime was a matter of general discussion when the Frys returned to London. St Mildred's Court opened off a street called Poultry.

Walking westward along it, Elizabeth could soon reach Newgate, the most infamous prison in England. Frequently she would have seen a scaffold draped in black outside the great gateway. Public executions were held there, and huge crowds would gather for the spectacle, while the deep prison bell tolled over London. Even when there was no scaffold erected, Newgate had a sinister allure. Groups of sightseers were usually standing outside, eyeing the gaunt stone walls, and recounting tales of notorious prisoners, riots, and daring escapes.

Close though she lived to Newgate, Elizabeth was not the sort of person to join the sightseers. Probably she had not thought much about prisons, until a young Quaker called Stephen Grellet arrived unexpectedly at St Mildred's Court.

Like William Savery, Grellet came from America. He was a descendant of French aristocrats, and was used to a comfortable life. The poverty and degradation which he saw in London horrified him. He felt a strong urge to do something about the wretched young criminals who roamed the streets with nobody to turn to for help. All they could expect, he heard, was to be locked up in some terrible prison. So Grellet asked to see the prisons for himself.

His experience of Newgate, on a cold January morning, drove him straight to Elizabeth's house. He needed the help of an active, caring woman, and presumably he had already met her, and knew what she had done at Plashet. He poured out his story to her. He had seen the women prisoners at Newgate, and

Women in Newgate Prison

their plight was desperate. Locked into a filthy quadrangle and adjoining rooms, they lay without bedding on the floor; and newborn babies, imprisoned with their mothers, had no clothes, and were freezing to death. Could Elizabeth do anything?

Elizabeth responded immediately. In no time she

had bought rolls of warm flannel, and collected a group of Quaker friends who were good needlewomen. They sewed all afternoon, and by evening a bundle of baby clothes was ready.

Next morning Elizabeth went with another woman to the prison governor, explained what had been done and asked to deliver the clothes herself. At first the governor refused. She had no idea, he said, what the women prisoners were like. The male prisoners were bad enough, but the women's quarters were known as 'Hell above ground'. The inmates would tear the clothes off a visitor's back, he warned. Even the gaolers entered in pairs.

Elizabeth persisted. She was not afraid, she told him. She was used to poor people. She would like to see the prisoners herself. Reluctantly the governor consented.

For all her brave words, Elizabeth was inwardly trembling. Perhaps she was thankful that she had once practised being brave in the Eleven-sided Room. A gaoler led her and her companion down a gloomy passage. The air smelled foul, and shrieks of fury rang out. About three hundred women were imprisoned in the south quadrangle, locked behind a barred gateway. As the visitors approached, some women hurled themselves madly against the bars, screaming for food, money, or freedom. Those in front were wrenched back by their hair, while others struggled for a better place. Beyond the gate, women quarrelled and fought, or lay moaning on the cold ground.

Elizabeth's one concession was to leave her watch with the gaoler. Then she asked him to unlock the gate,

Entering the south quadrangle at Newgate

and she and her friend stepped into the seething mob. At once it was clear what protection a Quaker dress gave. The flaunting of fine clothes would have enraged the women, but Elizabeth's plain costume, together with the expression of kindness and sympathy on her face, seemed to work a miracle of calm. Quietly she explained why she had come – and they listened. The babies must be cared for, she said. She had brought clothes.

Soon every baby was dressed, but that was clearly not enough. Back she came next day with clothing for the most destitute, and straw for bedding. 'The filth, the ferocious manners and expressions of the women towards each other, and the abandoned wickedness which everything bespoke, are quite indescribable,' she said afterwards. But, at the time, she managed not to show what she was feeling. Indeed, as she left at the end of her second visit, she paused, then dropped to her knees, and prayed aloud for the prisoners. They were absolutely silent, listening to those unexpected words on their behalf. Then quietly Elizabeth rose, signalled to the gaoler to open the gate, and walked back into the outside world.

She went home, bathed, and changed her clothes. But she could not change the pictures of Newgate, which filled her mind. All those women, from murderesses to poor mothers who had only stolen for their starving children, shut up together in one dirty courtyard and a few squalid rooms. There was work to be done, but for the moment it had to wait. The Gurneys had put money into the Frys' bank, and saved it. Elizabeth and Joe could go back to Plashet.

7 The Miracle

It was impossible for Elizabeth to forget Newgate, but while she was at Plashet there was nothing she could do about it. She went on as before, helping the poor people of the village, or hurrying to nurse sick relations. Her family might wish she were not so religious, but they relied on her kindness and practical ability whenever they were in trouble. There was an echo of her Newgate experience when she came home once to find the governess beating one of her children. Elizabeth detested violent punishment, and believed it was no way to right wrongs. The governess was dismissed.

Then, in 1816, the bank ran into more difficulties. There was now peace with France, but the war had wrecked the English economy. The Frys' bank could not meet the demands for money, and this time even the Gurneys could not help. Almost bankrupt themselves, Joe and Elizabeth had to cut their expenses drastically. They closed Plashet, sent their elder children to live with relations, and, back in St Mildred's Court, tried to adjust to a life of poverty. Partly as a distraction from her worries, partly because the reduced household gave her more time, but mainly because she had thought of something useful to do, Elizabeth returned to Newgate just after Christmas.

Since her last visit other people, including her brothers and two brothers-in-law, had become interested in prison conditions. They compiled reports, discussed theories of punishment, and planned possible new laws. While they talked, Elizabeth acted.

The numbers of women in Newgate were just as great, though a little more space had recently been allotted them. What worried Elizabeth were the children, imprisoned with their mothers because they had nowhere else to go. She thought of her school at Plashet, and her Imps at Earlham, and she made her plans. Trusting to the protection of her Quaker dress, she once more asked permission to enter the women's quarters.

She had half forgotten the smells, the darkness, and the ear-splitting shrieks. Struggling to calm her own fears – for the women, like animals, would sense fear, and react violently – she stepped through the barred gate. The screaming mob surged round. Two women were slashing each other with long fingernails; others howled an obscene song. On the ground amongst them, a little boy was sitting. Elizabeth picked him up, praying that her voice would be steady as she spoke.

'Friends,' she said, 'I too am a mother. Is there not something we can do for these innocent little ones?'

These unexpected words caught the women's attention. They listened.

'I have come,' said Elizabeth, 'to help you to start a school.'

The secret of Elizabeth's success with the prisoners

was that she never gave them orders. She treated them as reasonable human beings who would cooperate to improve their own conditions. Now they responded eagerly to the idea of a school. Elizabeth went back to the governor to ask for the use of a suitable room. Distrusting her as an impractical idealist, the governor answered that no room was available. Elizabeth discussed the problem with the prisoners. Could they think of a room somewhere? They could. They would give up

Women prisoners listen to Elizabeth reading from the Bible

one of the new common cells they had just been allocated. An educated young woman, imprisoned for stealing a watch, agreed to try some teaching. Elizabeth told the astonished governor that the school was ready to start.

The change which that school brought about in the 'Hell above ground' was hardly believable. For when the women saw the children beginning their lessons, they realised that they needed to be educated as well. Most of them were illiterate, and all were desperate for some way of passing the monotonous days of their imprisonment. To the alarm of the teacher they surrounded the schoolroom, begging to be allowed in.

Elizabeth was greatly in favour of their learning to read, and she thought that they should also learn to sew. In those days, when all clothes were made by hand, a needlewoman could always find employment. If a prisoner left Newgate able to earn her living, she would be less likely to return to crime. In fact, as Elizabeth quickly saw, classes for the women were just as important as classes for the children.

She had formed a Ladies' Committee to help her, and members of this committee now began going daily to the prison with books and sewing materials. They showed the prisoners how to cut out and stitch clothes for themselves and their children. A strange, purposeful hush fell over the south quadrangle.

As the schools settled down, Elizabeth and the prisoners drew up rules together. They worked in groups of twelve with a monitor, chosen from the best-behaved women, to supervise each group. Before they started, they had to wash their hands and faces, and put on clean blue aprons. All day they worked, and at six in the evening they gathered in a large room, and sat quietly in rows, while Elizabeth read the Bible aloud, and explained its meaning in her clear, gentle voice. The women loved the stories, and their tensions relaxed under the spell of Elizabeth's kindness. Instinctively she identified with them. When she spoke of Christian behaviour, she always said, 'We must do this', never 'You must'.

Once her system was working properly, Elizabeth applied to the London Corporation to have her school recognised officially as part of the prison. If it was, she could be confident it would go on running, even when voluntary help was not available. The Lord Mayor asked to visit the school, and arrived with his aldermen. They could hardly believe what they saw. Instead of the usual turmoil, there were the notorious women prisoners sitting quietly, listening to the Bible.

Elizabeth writing in her diary

They couldn't keep quiet about what they had seen. It was too amazing. The news of the Newgate miracle spread swiftly through London. The name of Elizabeth Fry, unknown a few days earlier, was on everyone's lips. Who was she? What was she doing? Other people appeared at Newgate, demanding to see this marvel for themselves.

Elizabeth had to make an important decision. Was it better to damp down curiosity, or give publicity to her own achievement? She hadn't gone to Newgate looking for fame; indeed she feared that, if people praised her, she might become too proud. But, after thought and prayer, she determined to make the Bible reading times open to selected visitors. It would encourage the once despised women if their conduct met with approval, she thought; and it might lead to improvements in other prisons. So she began to allow people of influence to mingle with the convicts, while she read aloud to them all.

'I have seen the two greatest sights in London,' the American ambassador wrote home, 'St Paul's Cathedral, and Elizabeth Fry reading to the prisoners in Newgate.'

And Elizabeth wrote in her diary, 'I have found in my attention to Newgate a peace and prosperity that I seldom, if ever, remember to have felt before.' So many of her relationships – with her sisters, her husband, and her children – had been disappointing. The prisoners made a family with whom she could be completely happy. William Savery's teaching about love and brotherhood, and Deborah Darby's prophecy, had both found fulfilment in Newgate.

8 Execution and Transportation

As she passed in and out of Newgate, Elizabeth found time to talk to individual prisoners. She tried to encourage them to look forward to the future, not back to their crimes, and to plan for a new way of life after their release. But this was not always possible; some of the women were under sentence of death.

Most women were quite unable to face the ordeal of public execution calmly. Naturally they knew what lay ahead. Everyone in Newgate talked about it. With their arms tied to their sides, they were led out onto the black-draped scaffold. The street below was filled with an excited crowd, jostling for the best view, while privileged spectators watched from their own stand. With hundreds of eyes upon them, and with jeers and hoots ringing in their ears, the condemned women felt the noose encircle their necks, and the trapdoor give way under their feet. They could only hope that death would follow instantly.

Tension rose in the prison as an execution date approached. Some of the women awaiting death became so frenzied, they had to be confined in a strait-jacket.

Elizabeth went into Newgate one day in May 1817, and found the south quadrangle in an uproar. A woman

Elizabeth comforts the condemned woman

called Elizabeth Fricker was due to hang next morning. At her trial she was accused of letting a burglar into the house where she worked as a servant, and the penalty for aiding a burglary was death. The thief himself had already been executed, but the night before he died, he confessed that Elizabeth Fricker had not opened the door. Someone else had let him in. But in spite of this nearly conclusive proof of her innocence, the authorities would not reconsider the case. She had been condemned to die, and die she must.

Naturally she was almost frantic. Elizabeth Fry sat with her, reading, praying, holding her cold hands, and gradually giving her the courage to face her unjust death. The horror of the occasion imprinted itself deeply on Elizabeth's mind, and she became a determined opponent of the death penalty.

The excessive use of capital punishment for fairly

minor crimes was beginning to have an effect on public opinion. Enlightened people made speeches, or wrote newspaper articles against it. Elizabeth strongly supported the campaign; but, as usual, while others spoke and argued, she preferred direct action. So when, in March 1818, a young woman in Newgate called Harriet Skelton was condemned to death for using forged banknotes which her husband had given her, Elizabeth went personally to the Tory Home Secretary, Lord Sidmouth, to appeal for mercy.

Once again there were good grounds for a reprieve. Harriet probably didn't know that the notes were forged. Elizabeth presented her case with confidence. But Lord Sidmouth was an obstinate, reactionary man. He hated any pressure for change or reform, and he knew Elizabeth's reputation as a prison reformer. He flatly turned down her plea. Full of indignation, Elizabeth hurried to an old acquaintance of Earlham days, Prince William. He sympathised with her cause, and spoke to Lord Sidmouth himself. But Sidmouth,

Lord Sidmouth

declaring that 'Mrs Fry had tried him exceedingly', wouldn't budge, and another innocent woman was executed.

It was easy for Elizabeth to over-estimate her own influence at this time. She had gained a tremendous popular reputation. She had given evidence on prisons to a Parliamentary Committee. The Queen had asked to meet her, and inquired if she wasn't afraid of going into Newgate. But gratifying though these occasions were, they did not mean that Elizabeth had any power to influence policies. Sorrowfully she left the campaigning to men, and returned to her woman's sphere of practical action. Another aspect of punishment had caught her attention.

People convicted of serious crimes who were not hanged, were often sentenced to transportation. They were put onto boats in the Thames or the Channel, which sailed for Australia once they had the required number of prisoners on board. The ships zigzagged across the Atlantic, to Rio de Janeiro, back to Capetown, and on through the sweltering Indian Ocean, reaching Botany Bay after a four or five months' voyage. For much of the time the convicts were kept in holds below the decks. In stormy weather water seeped through the sides of the ships, soaking the bedding. Often they were becalmed in the tropics, and then the heat and smells became almost unbearable, while water was strictly rationed. Weakened by the rigours of the journey, the women were put ashore in Australia, with no means of supporting themselves except by begging.

The problem of the convict ships came to Elizabeth's

notice in the summer of 1818, when the usually orderly south quadrangle erupted into one of its old riots. A group of women were to be transported next day, and, in wild rebellion, they were trying to break up the prison. At that moment, the prospect of Australia frightened them less than what would happen next day. Prisoners for transportation were chained together, loaded into open carts, and driven through shricking crowds to the river.

Elizabeth went straight to the governor, and pointed out the horrors of the chains and open carts. If he would allow the women to travel unchained, in closed carriages, she would calm the riot. By now the governor trusted her, and he agreed. Elizabeth gathered the women, and explained what she had done. At once the disturbance died down, and next morning the convicted women stepped quietly into their closed carriages.

But what could she do about the convict ships themselves? They, she decided, must be reorganised on the pattern of Newgate. She boarded the ship with the women, and described her plan to the captain, who willingly agreed to anything that would make his job easier. Captains seldom enjoyed transporting a load of convicts.

Elizabeth found a small space where the prisoners' children could do their lessons. Then she divided the women into the familiar groups of twelve, and gave them all materials to make patchwork quilts. They could sell the quilts in the ports where the ship docked, and use the money to support themselves until they found work in Australia.

Manacled women boarding a convict ship

For the next twenty years, Elizabeth inspected almost every convict ship which sailed from London, to ensure that her arrangements would be carried out. She, and her Ladies' Committee, provided every woman prisoner with a bag containing pins, needles, coloured thread, thimbles, scissors, and two pounds of patchwork pieces, as well as spectacles for those who needed them, and a comb, knife, fork and spoon of their own. She saw that there were books on board, and asked for them to be handed out as rewards for good behaviour.

So the same transformation which had happened at Newgate, took place on the convict ships. Bored and miserable women, fighting and quarrelling, no longer troubled the captain. Instead the prisoners stitched industriously, and landed in Botany Bay with money in their pockets, and a new sense of self-respect. It was still dreadful to be separated from their families, and sent halfway across the world; but now they had the hope that they might one day be able to buy their passage home.

9 The Prisoners' Friend

In the 1820s and 1830s Elizabeth Fry was famous as the world's leading expert on prisons. Prison authorities, first in Britain, and then all over Europe, begged her to visit them, and advise on improvements. Elizabeth never refused such an invitation. Exhausting though it was to travel the rough, dusty roads in a horsedrawn carriage, she was sure it was her duty.

When she reached a prison, she inspected every corner, talked to the gaolers, and, even more, to the prisoners, and then made her recommendations. Rehabilitation and not punishment was always her aim. Convicts were no longer chained to walls, but given employment, and Ladies' Committees were formed to help and encourage women prisoners.

When she spoke at public meetings, crowds came to hear her. When she travelled abroad, Kings and Queens received her as an honoured guest. She had become, quite simply, the best-known woman in England.

Those courtly manners, of which the Frys had complained, suited her as a celebrity. She was a stately figure in her high Quaker cap. She had a dignity which made people respect her views – most people, at least. But all her fame did not compensate for her continuing problems with her family and her fellow Quakers.

Throughout her adult life Elizabeth had lived as a committed Quaker. She only missed Sunday meetings if she was unwell. She wore Quaker clothes, used Quaker speech, and conformed to Quaker customs even when it went against the grain. Quakers believed that all people were equal, so there was no need to pay special respect to anyone. This meant that, when Elizabeth met the Queen, it was the Queen, not Elizabeth, who dropped the polite curtsey. Yet for all her faithfulness, she was not liked by the Quakers. They resented her eminence, they accused her of worldliness when she mixed with important people, and made endless criticisms of the way she managed her family. They said that if she stayed at home more, instead of gadding ostentatiously about, her husband and children would be better Quakers.

Early in their married life, Elizabeth and Joe had

A Sunday meeting

somehow lost contact with each other. In those hectic years at St Mildred's Court, there had been no time for them to adapt to each other. Joe had kept his promise. Elizabeth had far greater freedom than most married women, and Joe was often generous with his money. But he was a poor businessman. After years of financial insecurity, he went finally and irrevocably bankrupt in 1828. Once again the Gurneys provided help, but it was galling for Joe and Elizabeth to be always poor relations, dependent on charitable hand-outs. Sometimes Joe must have felt completely dominated by the Gurneys, with their money and their advice.

It was a Quaker rule that bankrupts should be expelled from membership, and Joe was not spared this humiliation, in spite of his wife's fame. Some Quakers probably enjoyed the chance to humiliate Elizabeth through Joe. As a result he gave up even a pretence of interest in Quaker affairs. He threw away his plain coats, and revelled in pleasures he had previously denied himself.

The fact that all her children rejected Quakerism was a bitter disappointment to Elizabeth. She had eleven children altogether, giving birth to the last one on the same day as her second daughter had her first baby. Elizabeth loved them dearly, but she never learned the art of managing them. They disliked Quaker meetings as much as young Betsy had disliked 'Goats', but she couldn't see the similarity. She forgot that she had chosen to be a plain Quaker only after she had had a lively social life, and failed to realise that her children too wanted a free choice. When she forbade them to go to parties, they grew rude and resentful. 'An unpolished family,' commented the contemporary writer, Maria Edgeworth, which was odd when Elizabeth had been blamed for having too much polish.

All her daughters, except the eldest who never married, had church weddings, which Quaker rules did not allow Elizabeth to attend. Joe went, but she stayed at home, stifling her disappointment, and writing each daughter as kind a letter as she could manage.

For more than twenty years she travelled vast distances in the cause of prison reform, and by 1843 she was exhausted. She had often been ill, and had only kept going with increasing doses of laudanum. Now her health deteriorated rapidly.

She had more than regrets for her husband and children to sadden her. A Prison Inspectors' Report on Newgate had attacked all that she had done there. She and her Ladies' Committee were criticized as well-meaning but foolish amateurs, and told that their visits 'diminished the necessary gloom of the prison, and mitigated the punishment which the law had sentenced the prisoners to undergo'. The Inspectors had even tried to stop Elizabeth's readings, and though they failed in this, it was clear that her humane ideals were doomed. New systems of imprisonment were coming into favour. It was thought that prisoners should be kept in solitary confinement, and new prisons were built with dark, single cells to provide the 'necessary gloom'. To Elizabeth they seemed far worse than the old communal rooms and yards of Newgate. She hated the idea of human beings locked up with nothing to see, and nobody to talk to.

In her last years she began to dream again. She had nightmares of graves opening all round her. Already she had lost brothers and sisters, children and grandchildren in death. Old beliefs were crumbling too. At last she saw that she had been mistaken in imposing Quaker disciplines on her unwilling children. The wearing of Quaker clothes and the use of Quaker speech were unimportant. To be guided by the Holy Spirit was all that mattered. She realised that this was what she should have taught her family, but she had failed, as it seemed her prison work had failed too.

Other people did not regard her as a failure. 'She was the only really great human being I have ever met with whom it was impossible to be disappointed', wrote the Duke of Argyll. 'Her eyes were calm, wise and steady, and she had an expression of sweetness, dignity and power.' Baron de Bunsen wrote more simply – 'Mrs Fry, my favourite saint.'

When she died after a stroke on 13 October 1845, her funeral was held at the Quaker burial ground in Barking. The news of her death had spread through London, and the streets of Barking were thronged with people. 'There were a great many of the most notorious London thieves,' wrote her daughter Katharine, 'who had come out of respect for her who had done so much for them.' The police refused to allow any known criminals into the burial ground, but they stood outside in the cold autumn wind, and mourned for Elizabeth Fry.